How to Draw

People

For Jesse, Jasmine, Justin, Jordan, Melina, and Matthew

Published in the United States of America by The Child's World®
PO Box 326 • Chanhassen, MN 55317-0326
800-599-READ • www.childsworld.com

Acknowledgments
Illustration and Design: Rob Court
Production: The Creative Spark, San Juan Capistrano, CA

Registration

Library of Congress Cataloging-in-Publication Data
Court, Rob, 1956–
  How to draw people / by Rob Court.
    p. cm. — (Doodle books)
  ISBN-13: 978-1-59296-809-1 (library bound : alk. paper)
  ISBN-10: 1-59296-809-0 (library bound : alk. paper)
  1. Human figure in art—Juvenile literature. 2. Drawing—Technique—Juvenile
literature. I. Title. II. Series.

NC765.C68 2007
743.4—dc22
                                2006031563

The Scribbles Institute™

Doodle BOOKS™

How to Draw

People

by Rob Court

The Child's World®

1

2

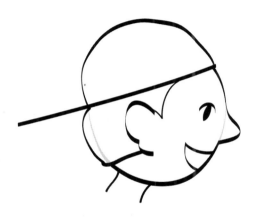

3

4

pilot

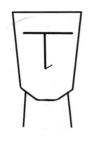

1

2

3

4

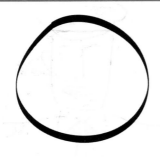

1

2

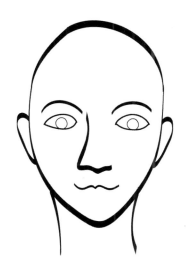

3

4

chef

1

2

3

4

dentist

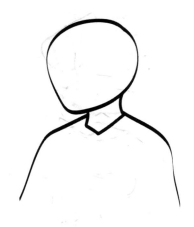

1

2

3

4

small boy

1

2

3

4

1

2

3

4

astronaut

1

2

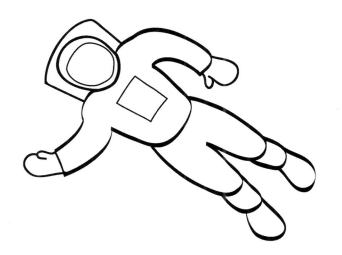

3

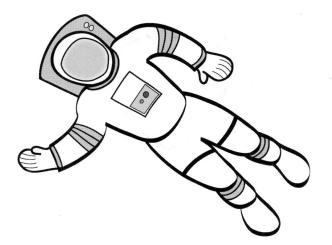

4

veterinarian

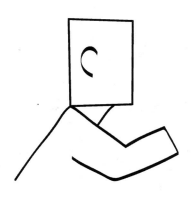

1

2

soccer player

1

2

3

4

police officer

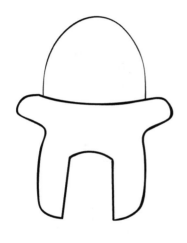

1

2

3

4

firefighter

1

2

3

4

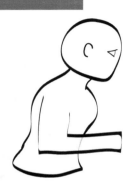

1

2

3

4

doctor

1

2

3

4

lines

horizontal

vertical

angled

curved

thick

thin

.... dotted

squiggly

dashed

point

Move a point
to make a line.

Connect lines
to make a shape.

Shapes make all kinds
of wonderful things!

loop

Repeating dots,
lines, and shapes
makes patterns.

About the Author

Rob Court is a graphic artist and illustrator. He started the Scribbles
Institute to help students, parents, and teachers learn about drawing
and visual art. Please visit www.scribblesinstitute.com